Singularity

Lizzie Austen

Ukiyoto Publishing

All global publishing rights are held by

Ukiyoto Publishing

Published in 2022

Content Copyright © Lizzie Austen

ISBN 9789356452305

*All rights reserved.
No part of this publication may be reproduced,
transmitted, or stored in a retrieval system, in any
form by any means, electronic, mechanical,
photocopying, recording or otherwise, without the
prior permission of the publisher.*

The moral rights of the authors have been asserted.

*This is a work of fiction. Names, characters,
businesses, places, events, locales, and incidents are
either the products of the author's imagination or
used in a fictitious manner. Any resemblance to
actual persons, living or dead, or actual events is
purely coincidental.
This book is sold subject to the condition that it shall
not by way of trade or otherwise, be lent, resold,
hired out or otherwise circulated, without the
publisher's prior consent, in any form of binding or
cover other than that in which it is published.*

Contents

The Butterfly Nebula	1
Pedal Pushers	2
Beautifully Cursed Appendage	4
Amplified	6
Bird's-eye View	7
Heroes of Papyrus	9
Paintero*	11
Verdant	14
Venus Flytrap	15
Profound at Nineteen	16
Morrow	18
Love of Yore	19
Que, sera, sera	20
Glory Cedar	21
Rustic	22
We See Red	23
Providence	24
Treacherous Hearts	25
Hoodwinked	26
Zarathustra's Mark	28

Hard- Boiled Hearbeats	30
Outlier	32
The Big Bad Wolf	34
Upside Down	36
Moth to a Flame	37
Once Upon a Pipe Dream	39
Absolute than Kismet	41
Yin and Yang	42
Memento for a Special Girl	43
Queens of Themyscira	46
Abysmal	48
Kaleidoscope	50
A Writer's Oasis	52
Epilogue	53
About the Author	*54*

The Butterfly Nebula

You are one story yet to be told,
Mighty highs and lows,
Here we stumble and go.
Rise up, up, up, with the stars,
There you will see
How far you've come.
When asterisks no longer matter,
You put them on pedestals.
Crying on crystals,
You remain strong, indomitable,
Each milestone carves one heart,
Too stiff, too kind–
What else can you do to make it better?
Write a letter?
Or jump to another dimension?
Oh, sweet lady,
Where you go is where you will meet your destiny.

Pedal Pushers

Tick, tick, click,
The wheels are ready.
You follow the trail–
Up, up, up,
Down, down, down,
The mountains and seas.

You crane your neck
For the road ahead.
Loud horns, cricket noises,
Accompany you to the edge
Of every summit or pitfall.

Each push of your feet,
Each turn of your handlebar,
Makes your heart happier than ever,
For what is life without adventure?

Lizzie Austen

When you reach the zenith,

Don't be afraid to look down;

See the earth from the rise,

With your bicycle–

You can do anything,

Go anywhere you want.

Pedal pushers will help you

Look what's yonder,

Point a place in the map,

So I can look for you down under.

Beautifully Cursed Appendage

Beautifully Cursed Appendage
A dragonfly once perched
On a windowsill.
Its wings fluttered, lurched,
Grew silent as it searched for its meal.
Once it flew from a farm field,
Bringing with it a strip of light
To the Farmer's Guild.
Who else would want a dark dragonfly?
Unbeknownst to its companions,
It carried a broken wing
For far longer than a millennium.
Yet it thrived, flew past lakes,
From cornfields to rose gardens.
Purified with the sight,
Its round eyes afforded

What any other dragonfly couldn't see.

Panoramas of blurry nature

Made it dance in glee,

If only, if only,

Everyone had the power to see,

It would never trade

Its black, broken wing,

Even for a beautiful tree.

Amplified

My mind keeps ticking;

It's louder than any bell.

Wired differently from birth,

We can see

How unique are we.

Our thoughts are dominoes;

They move sinuously

From one point to another,

Or perhaps from one person to the other?

What does it feel like?

To cry,

To say goodbye,

To move in synch,

With people we feel closest to,

With moments we lost hope to.

Our thoughts are codes;

They scream to fight turpitude;

They sing songs to lure us from our humble abodes.

Lizzie Austen

Bird's-eye View

The sky lights up with a thousand eyes
Staring at you from above.
Stars, planets, asteroids,
All wait for you to–
Look up,
Smile, laugh,
Or even cry.
You whispered to me once
The mysteries of the universe.
What happens inside a black hole?
What makes up dark matter?
How the universe started
Makes the scientists go mad.
You laughed and said,
They are fools
For playing gods.
It is enough if you die
Without seeing the multiverse.

You will be happy in your death
When another star is named.
These breakthroughs don't matter to you;
To get a glimpse of them
Through the naked eye
Is the greatest gift of all.

Lizzie Austen

Heroes of Papyrus

I once adored a boy
Made of words and metaphors.
He's not a cookie-cutter–
For the ships he sailed,
For the wars he fought,
For the planes he flew in Adriatic Sea.

If you look too closely,
You will realize that
He's the brother you haven't seen in ages.
He's the neighbor who helped you
When no one else didn't offer a thing.
He's a stranger you thought was bad
When, in fact, he meant to do good.

Heroes of papyrus aren't paper-thin
Nor are they figments of a desperate,
Moony-eyed artist.

They feed a hungry heart,
From poets to novelists.
Generations after generations,
Piles of ink blotted
And spilled for building these heroes.

Alas! I made a mistake.
Does life imitate art?
Or does art imitate life?

Paintero*

It was the fifth week of summer,
July of the late nineteen ninety-nine,
In a muddy rice field
Behind Grandma's home we played,
Skipped stones, picked flowers,
Their petals uglier than their thorns.

My friends beckoned me to join,
But I shook my head, stuttered,
Heard my stomach grumble.
You shan't join,
It said.
You don't belong there,
It whispered.

My gut was right;
They did leave me without further ado.

From there I began to wonder,
If my only solace was
Under the trees of mango.
I swore
I would never miss that moment
When I grew up.

I was wrong;
Something drew me in.
It crashed, pulled me
To that moment
When the winner takes it all.
I couldn't fathom the joy it must have felt
For I wasn't there–
To join in their soaring win,
To be that kid once again,
To not know what lies ahead,
And what will become of me.

Patintero is a traditional children's game usually played outdoors. *Patintero* is derived from the Spanish word *tinte* ("*tint*" or "*ink*") in reference to the grid lines commonly drawn by wetting the ground with water.

Verdant

I had a dream so teal
little girls in their tutus
walked past with their hair pale
against the midday sun.

I hurried across
the pavilion to see-
on the boardwalk
crowds gather
around a verdant semi-circle;
they dance, sing, and laugh.

Venus Flytrap

o'er your slimy leaf I crawled;
sweet nectar, so inviting,
your luscious teeth were waiting,
snap trap, what a booby trap!

sharp bristles caught me
in one embrace;
i was swallowed, unfazed,
in one sharpless toothy gulp!

the countdown began
like any other-
one pause,
two side to sides,
three kisses,
now I want to hide!

Profound at Nineteen

like an hourglass,
our story began in minutiae.

like blacksmiths forging metals,
we must keep these
feelings at bay.

what ifs turn to how are yous,
enemies to lovers to beaus.

alas! confidence strengthens us;
you and me together
in a sea of fuss.

mountain climbs, rocky shores,
snorkeling, uphill cycles.

slowly but surely,

a bond forges within,

profound at nineteen.

Morrow

champagnes of yesterday,
cheap red wines of today,
i'll wait 'til the morrow.

our sorrows come full circle,
anxiety leaps in a throttle,
i'll pause 'til our embrace.

tomorrow, we'll see
what it means to be free;
i'll stay 'til we meet.

Love of Yore

I

how do I taste thee?
beet red lips, sweet as berries
puckered in response
when I spoke epiphanies
how do I declare such love?

II

quit the tease thine love
lo! don't follow me yonder
where eyes lurk behind
sequoias bathed in moonshine
come, let us tarry instead.

Que, sera, sera

quiet is loud
can you see-
how owls stalk their prey?
why spiders weave every day?
only in tranquil
a self can be found.

que sera, sera
this life is ours!
why settle for one era
if you can live for all hours?

que sera, sera
one span of a decade
'tis short if well-played.

Glory Cedar

madre de cacao

mahamot mo na bulak

maberdeng dahon

nami sa akon mata

katahum 'di malimtan.

***glory cedar** is a tanka (31-syllabic Japanese poem) written in a local dialect. Endemic in some parts of the tropics, this beautiful plant has bright pink to lilac flowers that are tinged with white.*

Rustic

lo! look at thy eyes, wanderer!
cows grazing,
tamaraws bowing
under the sun's heat,
no farmer can't beat.

would you prefer the
noise of a bustling metro?
would you rejoice at
the smell of daisies
in the meadow?

'tis nature's way of paradox
in each equinox-
rustic countrysides stay
the same, I'd choose a sun's ray
o'er any other.

We See Red

banish from my thoughts!
oh dear, what did I do?
oh darling, what did you do?

like baneberries,
hate spat fire to our love
dust to must, we crumbled.

shook me from my dream!
lest it turned to nightmares,
lest demons breathe
once more.

farewell thee, sprinkles!
I bid thou bitter byes.

Providence

piercing gaze, so enticing,
come closer so
i can see what you're hiding.

do you not know?
your late Wednesday nights
hide your teen lovers
in a burrow.

darling, this rabbit hole unfurls
in a sudden revelation
don't make me find
your other girls.

Treacherous Hearts

try as I might,
your betrayal sliced through
with nothing but fright.

what can I do?
this wound brought pain
so skin-deep
lacerations not few.

undid, fastened to
your love like a kite,
i'm a fool to a promise for two.

Hoodwinked

Come hither, sly cunning fox,
Your mask slips when no one's looking,
Words of affirmation, so orthodox,
Everyone draws near when you're howling.

You met me when my sorrow was deepest,
Tamed me like other foxes;
I followed without protest,
'Til the day I realized your hoaxes.

Come on, you love me when I beg,
Come on, you love to judge the weak,
Unencumbered, naïve, tiny foxes.
Who can understand but you?
Who else but you can comfort us?

Give me one more wink, crinkle, tickle,
Sloe-eyed, so sweet, such deceit,

A demon spawn, a fallen angel,

Tell me, sly cunning fox,

Are you what you really are?

Zarathustra's Mark

Spirit of fire, heart like a stone,
Such is a man named Zarathustra.
Old in the soul, always alone,
Searching for wisdom in plethora.

He climbs down the mountains,
Bids valediction to his solitude.
Deep in the lowlands, lashing rains,
Unfettered with the steep altitude.

Zarathustra arrives in town,
Heart full, mind agog,
Only to see the meltdowns,
Frowns, murmurs, and hiss.

The people demand his judgments,
Ubermensch! *Ubermensch*!
Each with growing temperaments,

Are they chaos or dancing stars?

Zarathustra mounts his steed,
Indeed, a fellow knight will say,
Oh, lad! Tell us what you did.
There on the mountains, away from fray.

He speaks for the crowd,
Naysayers clamor for noises,
They mock, cluck, rock
Their heels and voices.

Silence plummets, hush descends,
Omnipresent Overman, Supreme Superman,
Live dangerously, he says, *plant the seed of your highest hope,*
Behold! Don't fret for I shall show you the Last Man.

Hard- Boiled Hearbeats

Call it dreaming, we linger along the edges
Of surreal. Lost in repentance

Against anything we've done wrong.
Polar opposites rarely do

Make a good match. Forces clash,
We both know how it ends–

Our laughter lost its luster, jokes turned
Sour. They left a bitter taste

On our mouths. Your hands reached for
Mine. 'Twas too late!

Open-ended tête-à-têtes forsook their tune.
Now we speak

In distant, lukewarm stares. Our paths began
To cleave as lightning would strike

The sky in white gray tendrils. Lovely paramour,
'Tis a love of rainbows to

Turmoil, turbulence, turgid tenacity.
'Tis no surprise we dig to

Look for rabbit holes. Will you be
Alright, darling? Will you

Succumb to your stolid state? Until when—
I dare ask—will our

Heartbeats cease? Will their rhythmic
Lub-Dubs turn to flatlines?

Outlier

Dainty lovely Missy
Unapologetic, false beauty,
A true-blooded know-it-all.

Willy peers in the dark, watching,
His mouth curls in disdain.
He rolls his eyes, scoffing–

She'll never be a wife to any man;
A lady shan't speak when hushed,
A lady shan't dress in a man's clothes.

Missy shall sing to him
In soft, sweet lullabies
To be the apple of his eyes.

Dissenter, outlier,
Eccentric, electric,

Lizzie Austen

No decent man will ever come.

What's there to see?
Missy's pert bosoms,
Skewed nose, ugly bottoms.

Willy furrows his brow;
Unladylike, so brash, such insolence!
Willy shakes his head without repent.

Drunk in prejudice, Willy perished
With his own noose wrapped around
His neck, thighs, hands unbound.

The curse dies with the tormentor,
Whilst Missy sails very deep, beyond the seas.
There! She'll be a woman of nobodies.

The Big Bad Wolf

I know you
You enslave women
With sugared words
Dipped in pixies of persuasion.

I know you
You're the man behind the mask
The animal hiding beneath the skin
Of a shy charming sheep.

I know you
You are blessed with wits
To conquer the innocent.

I know you
You whisper decadent songs
To lure women under your feet.

You are the Big Bad Wolf
You can take any shape
Any animal you want to morph into.

These girls you made your victims
They are not your playthings
They are humans
Blood, flesh, and bones
Built for the same purpose as you.

If you ever meet the Big Bad Wolf
Do not run
Do not fight
Listen to your gut
What does it say?
Fight or flight
The choice is yours.

Upside Down

A gamut of fear began to sprout
My darling, how could you?

Whilst you were away with your lover,
I sat among cypress trees and cower.

You turned me upside down,
With manicured nails, twisted frowns.

I handed sarcasm on a clean platter,
But you mistook it a blabber.

A wretched loss in my palate,
Oh dear mademoiselle, lest you forget.

Moth to a Flame

Why did you blame the moth
For being too arrogant,
Conceited to fly around the flame.
If you see it the other way
The moth mustn't be tamed
One attracts the wrong crowd
Jumping to conclusions
As Icarus would do the same
Sometimes words can only
Shadow what's behind the veil
Who are you hiding from?
What did you mean by that?
Questions linger around you
In incandescent murmurs.
When the moth's wings flutter close,
Take a step back,
Reinvent and peer closely,
Is it the moth or the flame?

Where does the fault lie?

Would you look again?

Whisper to me

Who needs a pregnant pause?

The moth or the flame?

Once Upon a Pipe Dream

Give or take,
that's what happens when you love,
or is it?

To like from afar,
to feel the tingle of nerves
traveling down your spine.

What did you see?
a happy mirage or tragedy?

Infatuation is only a trick,
a ruse of the brain's weird pathways.

This wishful thinking
will get you nowhere;
for who are you to like–
someone you can't reach?

someone you can't touch nor see?
someone your mind can only paint?

Absolute than Kismet

Two babes sprung

From two different wombs.

The fathers swear,

The mothers laugh,

It is but a miracle.

These two little angels will dance

When the clock strikes

At its decisive moment.

What will Cupid say?

Predestined or not,

When the time comes

For the stars and planets

To coalesce into one,

These two babes will understand

How and why the universe

Sees them as one.

Yin and Yang

Past, present, future
All blur into a void.
When I see you in déjà vus,
I'm reminded of hidden touches,
Moonlit kisses,
Dainty wishes.
If I could bring forth
These memories of you today,
I would build a monument
To honor our love
'Til the very last sprigs of May.
It is but a bumpy road ahead,
Full of patches,
Littered with wounds left untreated.
Will you take the chance again?
Will I accept you 'til the very end?

Memento for a Special Girl

You weren't there
When I first saw you.
Wise years will guide thee,
From this small Pacific Island
To the cornfields of Iowa,
Our hearts will follow.

Deep in my heart,
I know this bond will never break.
It's not unfair
To go away,
Life may demand more from us,
But we will still be the same.

Eight college girls
Who go crazy over
K-dramas,

Singularity

Fictional guys,
Smut books,
That's us.

I am happy and thankful
For meeting a friend like you.
Geography will not dare
Take us apart,
I can see the years beyond us,
Like ethereal, ephemeral dust.

You and I are still here,
No matter how distant
Our homes have become.
Store these memories for me–
Your quiet fire, elusive mire,
Independent, resplendent in any attire.

We will see each other again
Through space and time.
Life can be cruel sometimes,

But this gift of friendship
I will treasure for any dime.

Queens of Themyscira

Some say Wonder Woman
Belongs to the pretty popular.

I choose to differ;
They are everywhere–
Thick thighs, lush mouths,
Straight and curly hair,
Bodies wired for battle.

Some with feline eyes or ember voices,
Sparking fire when they speak.

Hear their lullabies,
Their lost hopes and far-fetched dreams.
When I see them from my past,
I will nod my head,
Even bow to them.

These queens of Themyscira I adore
For being brave, smart, and keen.

I will tell you this at once;
If you see a Wonder Woman,
Will you nod too?
Will you walk away?
Will you listen to her strength?

A Wonder Woman knows who she is,
Far more than those she loves least.

Skin, bones, and blood make up
Her wings. Beliefs and truths
Pump air to her lungs.
If she is a paradox,
Then what are you?

Abysmal

The mind dictates
While the heart follows.
You cannot betray me
With your absence.
My heart tore open,
When I saw you
Lying there,
Lifeless, eyes unmoving,
I cannot bear
To lose the rhythmic thump
Of a lively soul.
I clutched your hand,
Clammy and cold,
I shivered and drew you in.
Spice, smoke,
That's what you are to me.
You have left this world
Too abruptly,

Even I couldn't understand
Why the heavens have seemed
To punish us.
For years I have cried
Over what ifs and could have beens
We are both stained with passion
Deep down I know,
The heavens have sent you
For something grander than death.
You were a bitter pill to swallow,
Perhaps a beacon,
For my soul to follow
To another life.

Kaleidoscope

Visions of red and blue
I see you
In bits of mirrorlike images
Raven-haired
Glittering chocolate skin
I'd love to see it
Shine in the evening sun.

Each year
I could wish
A thousand symmetrical patterns
Of you in my mind
But what's left
Coalesce to shapes.

You're a bit of a parallelogram
Bent upon days of happiness
Failures and setbacks.

You're a pentagram
With your pointy stubborn streaks.

You're an oval
Forever catching thoughts
In a cycle of 365 days.

Your dreams have gathered
In a jar of shapes
Collected inside mirrors reflecting each other.

I'd love to see
Your lines, your angles.
In a kaleidoscope
I can only get a glimpse of the real you.

A Writer's Oasis

The cadence of words is sweet,
Honeyed and weaved through endless spins of time.

I can't remember when
But words speak to me
As if I can hear them soft and loud.

Some clash and break,
Others flow like a river.

Do you hear the voices of unsung stories?
They need to be told,
But is anyone around?

Epilogue

Poetry is a strange expression of thought compared to writing prose. When everything is at rest, you can hear the words forming–how they shape a verse into something profound and beautiful.

singularity is a different type of experimentation. Each poem reflects a state of mind. **singularity** can mean anything to any branch of knowledge. To physics, it's a state of infinity or the center of a black hole. In another context, it is used to describe something peculiar or something (or someone) behaving like a separate unit. For me, this word can mean anything to anyone. Much like when you're reading a poem or a book. To some, it's good and exhilarating; to others, it's predictable and boring. These tales are both real and illusory. As Stephen King once said, "The muses are ghosts, and sometimes they come uninvited."

To the person reading this, thank you for coming this far with me.

About the Author

Lizzie Austen

Born in the Philippines, Lizzie Austen comes from a small town with enough inspiration to fuel her writing. She holds a degree in Marketing and spends most of her time either in calligraphy or graphic design.

www.ingramcontent.com/pod-product-compliance
Lightning Source LLC
LaVergne TN
LVHW041225080526
838199LV00083B/3363